The Little Book of

Positivity

Felicity Forster

SIRIUS

This edition published in 2025 by Sirius Publishing, a division of Arcturus Publishing Limited,
26/27 Bickels Yard, 151–153 Bermondsey Street,
London SE1 3HA

Copyright © Arcturus Holdings Limited

All rights reserved. No part of this publication may be reproduced, stored in a retrieval system, or transmitted, in any form or by any means, electronic, mechanical, photocopying, recording or otherwise, without prior written permission in accordance with the provisions of the Copyright Act 1956 (as amended). Any person or persons who do any unauthorised act in relation to this publication may be liable to criminal prosecution and civil claims for damages.

ISBN: 978-1-3988-5829-9
AD012758NT

Printed in China

INTRODUCTION

Studies show a strong link between positivity and health, with positive people being better equipped to deal with stress and even recovering from illness more quickly. When we interact positively with other people, the feel-good chemical oxytocin is released in our brain, which improves mental wellbeing, resilience and performance.

Being optimistic doesn't mean ignoring our problems, though. It means that when challenges come, we assume that the best is going to happen rather than the worst. It's logical that if our thoughts are mostly negative, our outlook on life will be mostly pessimistic. So if our thoughts are mostly positive, we're more likely to have an optimistic outlook on life, and optimists tend to be healthier and happier.

Making small changes in our mindset can have amazing consequences, and the good news is that with practice we can all reframe situations and look on the bright side.

This little book of positivity is full of constructive reminders and exercises to help banish negative thinking and replace it with optimism. A helpful rule of thumb is: Don't say anything to yourself that you wouldn't say to a friend. Over time, you can learn to replace 'I've never done this before' with 'Here's an opportunity to learn something new', or replace 'This is impossible' with 'I'll do my very best to make this work'. Enjoy the quotes and positivity suggestions within the following pages, and keep asking yourself, is your glass half empty or half full?

'The best thing one can do when it is raining, is to let it rain.'

Henry Wadsworth Longfellow

'Keep your face always toward the sunshine – and shadows will fall behind you.'

Walt Whitman

Make
positive affirmations

Thinking positively about ourselves builds self-esteem and improves motivation. We all have worries and fears – often filling our heads at night – but we can learn to replace these negative thoughts with positive ones. Positive affirmations are short, simple statements, and when repeated often enough they challenge unhelpful thoughts and encourage positive change. Make a list and read it to yourself every day. Here are a few ideas:

❶ I am grateful for my life.

❷ My body is capable and my mind is strong.

❸ I am proud of myself.

❹ I am worthy of love and acceptance.

❺ I bring positivity to other people.

❻ Tomorrow is a fresh start and I will do my best.

❼ Wonderful things are going to happen to me.

'The greatest glory in living lies not in never failing, but in rising every time we fail.'

Nelson Mandela

'After all, the wrong road always leads somewhere.'

George Bernard Shaw

'We must accept finite disappointment but never lose infinite hope.'

Martin Luther King

Volunteer

Helping others has a hugely positive impact on our psychological wellbeing. It can give us a sense of purpose, increase our confidence, improve our social connections and broaden our skills.

❶ Research a range of charities and think about your passions. Are you interested in helping people, the environment or caring for animals, for example?

❷ Be realistic about how much time you can spare, and talk to other volunteers at the charity.

❸ Take part in community projects such as cleaning up parks, rivers or beaches, or helping out in a community garden.

❹ Sign up for fundraising activities to make money for charities. You could have a bake sale, a coffee morning, a raffle, a book sale or go on a charity run.

'Rule number one is, don't sweat the small stuff. Rule number two is, it's all small stuff.'

Robert Eliot

'Try to be a rainbow in someone else's cloud.'

Maya Angelou

'Do not anticipate trouble or worry about what may never happen. Keep in the sunlight.'

Benjamin Franklin

Love what you have

It's all too easy to notice the things we lack – a dream job, the perfect home, a supermodel's body – but unfortunately focusing on 'lack' tends to make us feel like failures. Instead of always making comparisons with other people and wanting more, if we could love what we already have, we'd find we have everything we need.

❶ Count your blessings in the present moment. Do you have a roof over your head, running water and food in the fridge?

❷ Whatever you're doing during the day, act with enthusiasm and intent. Do your best and engage with the people around you. As the saying goes, 'If you love what you do, you'll never work a day in your life.'

❸ Make a conscious habit of loving what you have, and your outlook on life will start to feel more positive.

'It will never rain roses: when we want to have more roses, we must plant more roses.'

George Eliot

'If you don't like the road you're walking, start paving another one.'

Dolly Parton

Plan a
holiday

Vacations feel more important than ever since the COVID restrictions, and research shows that planning a holiday can be almost as much fun as having one. Knowing that something good is just around the corner gives us something to look forward to and brings us feelings of positivity and excitement.

❶ Daydream about where you'd like to go – city, beach, mountains, island, country cottage, historical town?

❷ Talk about your planned trip. Sharing your ideas is part of the pleasure.

❸ Go online and look at photos and itineraries. The world is your oyster!

'But you will admit that it is a very good thing to be alive.'

L. Frank Baum

'Setting goals is the first step in turning the invisible into the visible.'

Tony Robbins

'Optimism is a happiness magnet.
If you stay positive, good
things and good people
will be drawn to you.'

Mary Lou Retton

Dive into nostalgia

Recalling happy memories from our past can renew our optimism, improve our self-esteem and give our lives a sense of meaning. Nostalgia can also help us connect with family and friends by giving us shared experiences to talk about.

❶ Rewatch movies that you enjoyed when you were younger. Re-experiencing those fondly remembered journeys with your favourite characters triggers all the feelings and emotions that you felt the first time.

❷ Sort out your photo collection. Make albums of special events or holidays so that you can revisit them whenever you need a pick-me-up.

❸ Recall the people who have been important in your life. If you have elderly relatives, connect with them and find out about your family history.

❹ Read old diaries, letters and cards.

'When things go wrong,
don't go with them.'

Elvis Presley

'You only live once, but if you do it right, once is enough.'

Mae West

'Carpe diem, seize the day boys,
make your lives extraordinary.'

N.H. Kleinbaum

Start a gratitude journal

Getting into the habit of writing down the things you're grateful for trains your brain to notice the positive things in life. The more you focus on positives, the more you'll find to enjoy and the happier you'll be.

❶ Buy a journal with a cover that you like, or use a gratitude app on your phone or tablet.

❷ Each day, write at least three things you feel grateful for.

❸ Rather than writing at random, it may help to set out some categories in advance. You could include pages for what happened during your day, what you saw, the activities you did and your social interactions.

'Every sunset is an opportunity to reset.'

Richie Norton

'Positive anything is better than negative nothing.'

Elbert Hubbard

'Hope is being able to see that there is light despite all of the darkness.'

Desmond Tutu

Cook

Instead of thinking of preparing food as a chore, cooking can be a hugely positive, creative and social activity that makes us feel good and becomes something we look forward to. Preparation tasks such as cutting, peeling, measuring and mixing can be a soothing form of meditation and mindfulness, and sharing a meal can be an expression of love and caring.

❶ Declutter your kitchen and perhaps play some relaxing music or listen to the radio.

❷ Start by cooking something that you love.

❸ Try new recipes. Your confidence will improve the more you practise.

'The grass is greener where you water it.'

Neil Barringham

'Learn from yesterday, live for today, hope for tomorrow.'

Albert Einstein

Celebrate and commemorate

Marking special occasions is good for our mental and physical wellbeing. When we celebrate significant milestones, we feel grateful and connected, and it feels good to be appreciated by others.

❶ Personal celebrations might include birthdays, weddings, anniversaries, starting a new job, paying off a loan, finishing a project or moving into a new home.

❷ There are plenty of official celebration days to enjoy throughout the year, such as St Patrick's Day, Mothering Sunday, Anzac Day, Independence Day, Thanksgiving, Hannukah, Christmas and New Year's.

❸ Other celebratory and commemoration days include Burns Night, Valentine's Day, the summer and winter solstices, Halloween and Remembrance Sunday.

'The way to make your dreams come true is to start believing in them.'

Helen Barry

'A No. 2 pencil and a dream can take you anywhere.'

Joyce Meyer

'I've had lots of troubles, so I write jolly tales.'

Louisa May Alcott

Listen to
music

Music can be a very powerful way to evoke positive emotions and memories. When we listen to an upbeat song or piece of music, it uplifts and energizes us, while soft, gentle music calms us down. Music can also be a prompt for evoking past emotions, reminding us of our parents, our youth, special holidays and significant life events.

❶ Choose lively music to make you feel happy. The right song usually makes you want to move!

❷ Sad songs and love songs have their place too. Listening to sad songs can help you get over break-ups and losses.

❸ Classical music can improve relaxation and make you feel emotional, and, according to some sources, even make you more intelligent.

❹ There are plenty of YouTube videos and apps that play ambient music to fit any mood.

'Waste no more time arguing what a good man should be. Be one.'

Marcus Aurelius

'Pessimism leads to weakness, optimism to power.'

William James

'When your back is to the wall and you are facing fear head on, the only way is forward and through it.'

Stephen Richards

Declutter
your home

Turning chaos into order brings feelings of calm, positivity and a sense of achievement. Living in a messy environment can make us feel stressed, anxious and out of control, so it's worth taking the time to keep our homes tidy and let go of things we don't need. Decluttering can be a mindfulness exercise in itself, and giving items to charity shops is beneficial to others.

1. Depending on how much clutter you have, it's may be easiest to start small – one shelf or cupboard, for example.

2. Create a decluttering box and fill it with odds and ends, items that make you sad and things you no longer use.

3. Go through your wardrobe. If you haven't worn something for a year or two, it's probably safe to add that to the box.

4. Avoid acquiring clutter in the first place by going paperless and resisting buying too many knick-knacks and ornaments. And when you do buy something new, donate its predecessor to charity.

'Don't waste a minute not being happy. If one window closes, run to the next window – or break down a door.'

Brooke Shields

'Life is too short for negativity.
Focus all your energy
to create happiness.'

Banani Ray

'When you are joyful, when you say yes to life and have fun and project positivity all around you, you become a sun in the center of every constellation, and people want to be near you.'

Shannon L. Alder

Listen to
your inner voice

Positivity can be found within when we learn to listen to our inner voice. We all have an inbuilt resilience – often more than we realize – and if we can tap into it, we can find the wisdom and strength to face life's challenges and problems.

❶ Sit quietly somewhere calm and comfortable for about 10 minutes. You may wish to light a candle or play soft background music.

❷ Think about a specific situation that is worrying you and ask yourself, 'What can I do to improve this situation?' or 'What will make me feel better right now?'

❸ Relax and let the questions rest in your mind.

❹ Pay attention to any ideas, thoughts, visions or feelings that come up. If any seem positive, explore them more deeply.

❺ Trust the answers you are giving yourself. Listen to your heart.

'You're braver than you believe, and stronger than you seem, and smarter than you think.'

A.A. Milne

'Each day comes bearing its gifts. Untie the ribbon.'

Ann Ruth Schabacker

Look after the environment

We can all make positive changes that will benefit our planet, helping with climate change and saving energy. The natural world sustains our very existence, so taking care of it is one of the most positive things we can ever do.

❶ When buying food, choose fresh, local ingredients as much as possible, and consider a more plant-based diet.

❷ Recycle, reuse and upcycle to reduce waste. Give unwanted items to charity shops.

❸ Conserve water and energy by turning off taps and lights when you're not using them. Consider using public transport, cycling or walking instead of driving.

❹ Grow your own vegetables and plant trees and flowers that attract pollinating insects.

❺ Volunteer for cleanups in your community and support environmental organizations.

'Those who don't believe in magic will never find it.'

Roald Dahl

'Speak your mind, even if your voice shakes.'

Maggie Kuhn

'It's a funny thing about life,
once you begin to take note of
the things you are grateful for,
you begin to lose sight of
the things that you lack.'

Germany Kent

Focus on your own growth

Breaking free from toxic patterns is often difficult, but one of the best ways of maintaining positivity is to work on our own personal growth. We can't control other people, but we can adjust the ways in which we respond to life's stresses and challenges.

1. Learn visualization and mindfulness techniques. Picture yourself solving problems or, if appropriate, walking away from them.

2. Reframe difficulties as challenges, don't think negatively and don't be afraid of failing. Failure can always be reframed as a learning exercise and an opportunity to try again.

3. Focus on your goals and how to achieve them. Always move forward with conviction and a positive attitude.

4. Believe in yourself and celebrate your victories. Even the smallest of triumphs will motivate you to keep going.

'In every day, there are 1,440 minutes. That means we have 1,440 daily opportunities to make a positive impact.'

Les Brown

'Your attitude is critical to success. If you expect things to be difficult, it will always be easier to solve problems, overcome adversity, and have an enthusiastic energy about how you go about and enjoy your work.'

Nick Saban

'I say looking on the bright side of life never killed anybody.'

Jenny Han

Manage
your time

Time is a limited resource – we all get the same 24 hours each day – so if we can learn how to manage it effectively, we'll feel many positive benefits. These may include increased focus and productivity, greater satisfaction, better self-esteem and reduced stress and anxiety.

❶ Plan your day, perhaps writing down a schedule of tasks that need doing. It often helps to write a 'to do' list the night before.

❷ Set down your goals, priorities and deadlines, and sometimes either say 'no' vor delegate to someone else.

❸ Take time off to boost your mental and physical health, and get plenty of sleep.

'Nothing is impossible,
the word itself says
"I'm possible."'

Audrey Hepburn

'Be yourself and people will like you.'

Jeff Kinney

'You know what's just as powerful as a good cup of coffee in the morning? Starting your day with some good, loving thoughts. It can change how your whole day unfolds.'

Karen Salmansohn

Be kind

One of the easiest ways to bring positivity into our lives is through kindness. Our positive thoughts and actions attract positive people and improve our feelings of wellbeing, while at the same time making others' lives a little brighter. Even the simplest of acts, such as holding a door open, can mean a lot.

❶ Show your gratitude to people around you. Say 'please' and 'thank you', smile at strangers and notice whenever someone acknowledges or helps you.

❷ Try to see the best in other people – give out compliments and high-fives!

❸ Be kind to yourself too. Many people are their own harshest critic; if you notice this, check yourself by following the rule of not saying anything to yourself that you wouldn't say to a friend.

'A dead end is just a good place to turn around.'

Naomi Judd

'It is better to dwell on the beautiful things in life than the negative.'

Lailah Gifty Akita

Practise
self-care

When we look after ourselves, we feel healthier and more positive. Self-care means making a range of healthy lifestyle choices, from eating well and keeping fit to taking care of our mental health and emotional wellbeing.

❶ Eat a balanced diet and drink plenty of water. You are what you eat!

❷ Aim to exercise for at least 30 minutes a day. This could mean a workout at the gym or going for a regular brisk walk.

❸ Pamper yourself by taking a relaxing bubble bath, booking a day at a spa or buying something nice for yourself.

❹ Nurture your mental health by doing things you enjoy, such as pursuing your hobbies and spending time with friends, family and pets.

'Extraordinary things are always hiding in places people never think to look.'

Jodi Picoult

'Be fanatically positive and militantly optimistic. If something is not to your liking, change your liking.'

Rick Steves

'You're going to go through tough times – that's life. But I say, "Nothing happens to you, it happens for you." See the positive in negative events.'

Joel Osteen

Do a digital declutter

Just as a cluttered home can make us feel stressed, the same is true of a cluttered phone or computer. Doing regular housekeeping on our digital devices is a positive step in restoring order, not to mention making our technology work more efficiently.

❶ Delete unwanted or duplicated pictures. As well as freeing up space, editing your photos regularly will also save time when viewing them later.

❷ Adjust your settings to minimize notification beeps, alerts, flags and pop-ups.

❸ Unsubscribe from mailing lists you don't need.

❹ Create clearly labelled folders for storing material so that you can find what you want quickly and easily.

❺ Sort and archive your emails daily.

'Success is a decision, not a gift.'

Steve Backley

'Be yourself, everyone else is already taken.'

Oscar Wilde

'To try is to invite uncertainty. Where confidence goes, success usually follows.'

Wayne Gerard Trotman

Manage stress and set boundaries

It's human nature to have worries, but have you ever heard the saying, 'Eighty-five per cent of what people worry about never happens'? Learning to manage stress and being clear with our boundaries are good strategies for keeping positive.

❶ Go with the flow and don't sweat the small stuff. It can help to ask yourself whether your present worry will still exist in a year's time. Some people take this to the extreme, arguing that *everything* is the small stuff!

❷ Arm yourself against stress by focusing on your strengths, managing your time effectively and taking frequent breaks. It can also be helpful to share your problems by chatting with someone you trust.

❸ Decide how much you're willing to tolerate. Communicate your boundaries clearly, and politely say 'no' when you reach your limit.

'Life's battles don't always go to the stronger or faster man. But sooner or later, the man who wins is the man who thinks he can.'

Vince Lombardi

'Elevate your inside game. A negative attitude is below the horizon . . . a place for lonesome hearts.'

T.F. Hodge

'Every strike brings me closer to a home run.'

Babe Ruth

Tune into the natural world

Spending time in nature makes us feel more positive, improves our mood and reduces feelings of anxiety and depression. Even just going for a short walk in the fresh air can make a difference.

1. Seek out green spaces and enjoy the scrunch of leaves under your feet and the breeze on your face.

2. Blue spaces also make us feel happier; these include the sea, rivers, streams, lakes, waterfalls and pools.

3. The natural world also includes all the animals, birds, fish and other creatures that live in it. Look for wildlife whenever you're out walking, or visit wildlife conservation parks or natural wetlands.

'Live life to the fullest, and focus on the positive.'

Matt Cameron

'Seeing the glass as half empty is more positive than seeing it as half full. Through such a lens the only choice is to pour more. That is righteous pessimism.'

Criss Jami

Look on the
bright side

There is a saying that 'When you focus on the good, the good gets better'. Once you learn to do this, you'll see positives in most situations and realize that every cloud actually does have a silver lining.

❶ Challenge your negative thought patterns. For example, instead of thinking 'I never do anything right', adjust this to 'Every day I am learning from my mistakes'.

❷ Reflect on past positive experiences and share stories about the 'good old days' with friends and family. Remembering good times is a great way of disrupting negative thoughts.

❸ Spend time with positive people. You'll find that positivity is contagious.

'Be the change that you wish to see in the world.'

Mahatma Gandhi

'Believe you can and you're halfway there.'

Theodore Roosevelt

'Make your life a masterpiece;
imagine no limitations on
what you can be, have or do.'

Brian Tracy

Stop catastrophizing

Sometimes our minds can leap to the assumption that the worst will happen in any situation. We may take a small event and magnify it so that our whole day is ruined, and unfortunately this can become a self-fulfilling prophecy. Learning to challenge and replace these unhelpful thought patterns can give us a more positive outlook.

❶ Accept that everyone has good days and bad days. But one bad day doesn't mean that every day will be bad.

❷ Whenever you notice yourself thinking negatively, say out loud, 'Stop!' to break your chain of thought.

❸ Schedule a worry session, allowing yourself a few minutes to think about your fears.

❹ Try to replace your negative thoughts with positive options instead. It may help to jot these down in a journal.

'The mind is not a vessel to be filled, but a fire to be kindled.'

Plutarch

'Enjoy the little things in life, for one day you may look back and realise they were the big things.'

Robert Bault

'You are your best thing.'

Toni Morrison

Engage in activities that bring you joy

Spending time doing the things we love feeds our mind with positive thoughts and emotions. Time seems to speed up when we're enjoying ourselves, and having fun is a great way to forget our troubles and cope with life's obstacles.

❶ Enjoy a good meal and savour every bite.

❷ Turn on your favourite music. Sing and dance around your home!

❸ Find a TV series that you enjoy and binge-watch it.

❹ Go on a trip, visit museums and art galleries, and take in new experiences.

❺ Enjoy the simple things too, like watching the seasons change.

'One of the things I learned the hard way was that it doesn't pay to get discouraged. Keeping busy and making optimism a way of life can restore your faith in yourself.'

Lucille Ball

'Once you replace negative thoughts with positive ones, you'll start having positive results.'

Willie Nelson

'Every morning you have two choices. Continue to sleep with your dreams, or wake up and chase them.'

Carmelo Anthony

Seek humour

Laughter can be a powerful drug, inducing positive changes in our physiology, lightening our mood and even reducing pain. Children laugh hundreds of times a day, but sometimes as adults we need to seek opportunities for humour.

❶ Go to a live comedy club or buy tickets to see a stand-up comedian.

❷ Watch comedy movies and TV shows, and look for funny videos on YouTube or social media.

❸ In your everyday life, try using humour to defuse tense situations.

❹ Arrange fun events with friends, such as karaoke, bowling or games nights.

❺ Check out the humour section in a bookshop.

'The most important thing is to try and inspire people so that they can be great in whatever they want to do.'

Kobe Bryant

'You can't stop the waves but you can learn to surf.'

Jon Kabat-Zinn

Practise
self-reflection

According to Socrates, 'The unexamined life is not worth living', so it's a good idea to check in with ourselves from time to time and keep track of the trajectory of our lives.

1 Identify negative thinking patterns. When something bad happens, do you automatically blame yourself or others? Either way, blame can cause us to get stuck. A more positive approach is to see situations as lessons to be learnt and help us grow.

2 Think about the past year and ask yourself the big questions. Do you enjoy your job? Is your relationship making you happy? Did you experience any milestones? Have you felt joy? Do you feel at peace and connected with the world? It's essential to be honest with yourself before you can start making positive changes.

3 Becoming more self-aware will give you greater control over your life and you'll be able to live the life you want and be the person you want to be.

'Trust yourself. You know more than you think you do.'

Benjamin Spock

'You can, you should, and if you're brave enough to start, you will.'

Stephen King

'I took a walk in the woods and came out taller than the trees.'

Henry David Thoreau

Let it go!

We often don't like change and it feels easier to hold on to established thought patterns and past ways of doing things, but when something no longer serves us, a more positive option is to let it go. This can give us the freedom and space to travel in a more positive direction in the future.

1. Declutter your mind with a 'brain dump'. This means writing down the contents of your mind on a blank sheet of paper. Spill out all your annoyances, stresses, worries and nagging thoughts, just as if you were emptying a bag.

2. Reach out to trusted friends, family members or mental health professionals, or join a support group. Talking and connecting with people helps us to feel understood and validated.

3. Tell the worry dolls! In Guatemalan tradition, tiny hand-crafted 'worry dolls' are given to anxious children. Before bed, the child tells their doll all their worries and fears, then puts the doll under their pillow; the next morning the child feels better. Adults can use worry dolls to relinquish their worries in exactly the same way.

'Success is falling nine times and getting up ten.'

Jon Bon Jovi

'**Say something positive, and you'll see something positive.**'

Jim Thompson